Tamp

Denton Loving's *Tamp* reminds us that to grieve is to love, a sacred act that aims for clarity, and yet, mourning, too, makes us acutely aware of the profound questions that agitate the living. Loving's poems, deeply attuned to the richness of a rural sacred order, both honor and attempt to name that complexity with a music that feels movingly restorative.

—Major Jackson, author of *The Absurd Man*

Each poem in *Tamp* is a world in its own right: each a timeless praise song to the earth, to solitude, loss, and love. With bucolic sensitivity shared by few, Loving has crafted the most convincing wake-up call—gentle, surefooted, hypnotic, and insistent. *Tamp* is a rare trove of honest, measured assurance, a blessed reminder of what matters most.

—Shawna Kay Rodenberg, author of *Kin: A Memoir*

In *Tamp*, his radiant new collection of odes and elegies, Denton Loving represents the works and days of rural Appalachia, and far beyond, with deep knowledge and delicate authenticity. Loving's poems occupy the ideal cross-section between two of poetry's oldest poles, the lyric and the narrative. It matters little whether readers greet these poems as stories that sing or lyrics that bind us in their telling, because the scenes and voices we discover will travel with us deep as treasured memories. I will never forget the image of the late father's missing gloves turning up in forgotten buckets long after his passing in "If There's an Angel for Lost Gloves." Galway Kinnell once said that another word for poetry could be "tenderness," and this is the quality Loving brings most acutely to the loved people and places he offers tribute in *Tamp*.

—Jesse Graves, author of *Merciful Days*

Also by Denton Loving

Crimes Against Birds

Seeking its Own Level: An Anthology of Writings about Water (editor)

TAMP

Denton Loving

MERCER UNIVERSITY PRESS

Macon, Georgia

MUP/ P661

© 2023 by Mercer University Press
Published by Mercer University Press
1501 Mercer University Drive
Macon, Georgia 31207
All rights reserved

27 26 25 24 23   5 4 3 2

Books published by Mercer University Press are printed on acid-free paper that
meets the requirements of the American National Standard for Information
Sciences—Permanence of Paper for Printed Library Materials.

Printed and bound in the United States.

This book is set in Adobe Garamond Pro.

Cover/jacket design by Burt&Burt.

ISBN   978-0-88146-673-1
Cataloging-in-Publication Data is available from the Library of Congress

LCCN   2023931605

for

Amy Marie Coffey Smith

1975-2022

MERCER UNIVERSITY PRESS

Endowed by

TOM WATSON BROWN
and
THE WATSON-BROWN FOUNDATION, INC.

Acknowledgments

The author gratefully acknowledges the following publications where poems in this collection first appeared, sometimes in slightly different form:

8 West Press ("Violet Iris"); *Adirondack Review* ("Genealogy" and "Standing on the Banks of the Tuckasegee"); *Anthology of Appalachian Writers, Dorothy Allison Volume* ("Play Where I'm Cast as Sycorax" and "Hurtling"); *Anti-Heroin Chic* ("Foundation," "On the Other Side of Wilderness," and "Unburied"); *Black Moon Magazine* ("After My Father Died, I Marveled," "Another River of the Underworld," and "Purification"); *Cider Press Review* ("Maelstrom"); *The Citron Review* ("Topography of Tears"); *The Czech Republic Ekphrastic Project* ("The Broken Man"); *The Coe Review* ("Balefire"); *Delta Poetry Review* ("South Through Kentucky" and "We Are Called to Reinvent Ourselves"); *Exit 7* ("Remembered by Name"); *The Good Men Project* ("Blue November"); *Harvard Divinity Bulletin* ("Hag Stone, Hex Stone, Holy Stone"); *Heartland Literary Magazine* ("Riding Lawn Mower"); *Heartland Review* ("Upon Meeting Judith Light in a Dream"); *Inscape* ("The Abacist"); *Kentucky Monthly* ("Copperhead"); *Kudzu Literary Journal* ("My Mother is the Green Mountains"); *Maryland Literary Review* ("If there's an angel of lost gloves"); *museum of americana* ("There is a barn"), *The National Poetry Review* ("The Fence Builder"); *One, the online literary journal of Jacar Press* ("The Mystery of the Hereafter"); *Peauxdunque Review* ("Fishing with the Saint"); *Pilgrimage Magazine* ("Fresh as an Asteraceae"); *Pittsburgh Poetry Review* ("Spring Signs"); *Swamp Ape Review* ("The Eyes of God"); *The Tishman Review* ("And You Too"); *Tributaries / The Fourth River* ("Learning to Drive")

"Roots" appeared in the poetry film by the same name, produced and directed by filmmaker Kevin Hillman through the Visible Poetry Project: https://vimeo.com/265974702

Contents

Foreword

Early in his writing career, an author advised Denton Loving to avoid poetry until he had mastered fiction. A discerning student compelled not to listen to such advice, Loving pursued the art of poetry as voraciously as that of prose.

Subsequently, Loving has come to know his craft and his material, and he mines it as his grandfather and great-grandfather once mined coal, that dark vein of heat and light. He climbs into the hard, cramped places, cutting deep below the obvious to what marries the natural world to the mythical, the body of family to the oversoul. Loving finds a seam of what is real and relevant and follows it until the payday of what is beyond real—what is revelatory. We saw evidence of this gift in Loving's *Crimes Against Birds*, a debut collection that does not read like the book of an emerging writer, but rather like that of a poet well-schooled and seasoned in his profession. We see that same power magnified in these pages of *Tamp*.

I have known Denton Loving since a time before he would have called himself a poet. In a visit he and I once had with a Pulitzer-Prize-nominated poet, Loving said, "I just don't know enough about poetry to say I'm a poet," to which the other poet responded encouragingly, "I don't know enough about poetry either. Nobody does." That desire to know enough drives Loving to explore, understand, and uncover hidden value in the world and the exceeding depth of his work. Draft after draft after draft, he returns to language, line breaks, metaphors, and allusions, and he worries them until the poem discovers itself. I have received numerous poems from him in draft form where the changes might be massive or subtle, but always the poem is improving and discovering itself because of the attention, patience, and focus Loving knows it requires. All the while, Loving is becoming the poet who can fully forge that particular flash of art.

For years, as a student, organizer, advocate, and teacher, Loving has been an instrumental member of the Appalachian writing community, particularly as a founding editor of *Drafthorse* literary journal and co-director of the Mountain Heritage Literary Festival, both based at Lincoln Memorial University, and a regular participant at the Appalachian Writers Workshop in Hindman, Kentucky. With his MFA from the Bennington Writing Seminars and his attendance at the Key West Writing Seminars and Sewanee Writers' Conference, Loving's community has grown to include numerous writers outside the mountains and beyond the South. He is now a founding editor of *Cutleaf* literary journal and Eastover Press. With every effort to help others, he has expanded his notion of what can be done both to encourage others and to continue one's own education. This generosity and openness provide their own rewards. In helping others, Loving also continually hones his own voice and dexterity on the page.

Always an insatiable reader, and now a masterful editor and inspiring teacher as well as an accomplished author, Loving has cultivated his skills as a writer across multiple genres and from a host of beneficial sources. As I read his poems, I am reminded of the work of Mary Oliver, Wendell Berry, Robert Morgan, Maurice Manning, Jesse Graves, Charles Wright and others—not to say the work is derivative in any way, but to say I feel the ancestry in Loving's work, that inheritance of gaze, its nurture from a lineage of accomplished and thoughtful poets who both respect the vernacular and pay "astonishing attention," as Ron Carlson puts it. As readers, we can share in the benefits of Loving's decisions, scholarship, and dedication to material and craft.

In his notes on poetry and craft, Theodore Roethke writes of the poet's intention, "Not only to perceive the single thing sharply: but to perceive the relationships between many things sharply perceived." That is also an apt description of poems herein, whether the poet allows us to perceive the thing and its relationships dead-on or through the softer lens of dreams. Herein lies the work's point of friction and source of energy, the liminal geography of language that broadens our understanding of whom and what we love and who and what loves us, no matter the root or effect, and how this understanding conjures and forges us into being. Particularly, Loving teaches us to explore the rough wilderness we are left with when our most defining relationship changes in a profound and irrevocable way.

Tamp, is a work of magic—not the cheap magic of sleight of hand or the familiar magic of fairytales, although these poems are written with a skillful hand, and tales unfold that include love, loss, yearning, and gorgeous acceptance at their heart.

Tamp is magic in the way fire is magic, the way a king of fire can exist and his wings be visible in the flaming flurry of October leaves coupled with the flight of small white-bellied birds. It is magic in the way a singularity is sorcery and stars its aftermath, the way language can live like an animal on the page, and a barn can be an honest-to-god ghost, rubbed smooth by all its living and dying. Magic is in the very word *tamp*: to pack, to set an explosive, to drive down with light or medium blows, to bury, to plant well, to shore up—as in a fence post standing beside bleached and scattered bones of named cows. Loving explores the intricacies and contrarieties of relationships where a fundamental grievance is also a matchless blessing, an unconditional love is always a lesson to be understood, a burden to carry, a puzzle to be worked, a place to lean against.

While Denton Loving tamps down his poems to their most essential spaces, at the same time, he "tear[s] the earth open" for love in their writing, and the poems that come from his efforts are alchemy.

—Darnell Arnoult
Mebane, North Carolina

Hurtling

I'm five again, and it's so dark I can't see
the road. *Are we going through a tunnel?*

My dead father says, *No. Go back to sleep.*
He reaches across the bench seat. The weight

of his hand quiets the starlings in my belly.
I know I'm safe as long as he's close.

Within the darkness, stars pinprick the horizon.
The small blue egg inside my breastbone

cracks with understanding: we're not sweeping
through a tunnel under the crush

of a mountain. We're hurtling across the heavens
on the wings of an ancient, magical bird.

I

Another River of the Underworld

In my dreams, I walk the banks
of an ancient, unnamed river
surrounding the island of my dead.
My heart is a boat with leaking ribs
beached on the river's far shore,
long abandoned by the ferryman.
I stand on the opposite side
of the water and try to recall
the four chambers of the ship
in the distance. I can only name
two: love and regret. So much else
remains obscure, but this I know:
sleep is another kind of prayer.

Genealogy

To be the son of a coal miner is to be a child of mountains
      and to be a child of mountains is to be Appalachian
and to be Appalachian is to be frontier & pioneer
      and to be frontier & pioneer is to be Boone's cousin
and to be Boone's cousin is to be longhunter
      and to be longhunter is to be tuckahoe & buckskin
and to be tuckahoe & buckskin is to be the son of Pocahontas
      and to be the son of Pocahontas is to be Powhatan
and to be Powhatan is to be tidewater
      and to be tidewater is to be settler & planter
and to be settler & planter is to be enslaved & enslaver
      and to be enslaved & enslaver is to be disinherited
and to be disinherited is to be a second son
      and to be a second son is to be Cavalier
and to be Cavalier is to be Catholic & Protestant
      and to be Catholic & Protestant is to lose your head
and to lose your head is to take a head or two
      and to take a head or two is to be Lancastrian & Yorkist
and to be Lancastrian & Yorkist is to be the devil's daughter
      and to be the devil's daughter is to be a friend of Dante
and to be a friend of Dante is to boil in the seventh circle
      and to boil in the seventh circle is to be a fratricide
and to be a fratricide is to be a king
      and to be a king is to wear a crown
and to wear a crown is to be a conqueror
      and to be a conqueror is to be a bastard
and to be a bastard is to be chosen by God
      and to be chosen by God is to be a saint
and to be a saint is to be a scourge & a plague

and to be a scourge & a plague is to be barbarian & pagan
and to be barbarian & pagan is to be the son of a bear
and to be the son of a bear is to be a senator
and to be a senator is to be a Roman imperialist
and to be a Roman imperialist is to be the twin son of a wolf
and to be the twin son of a wolf is to be an emperor
and to be an emperor is to be Julio-Claudian
and to be Julio-Claudian is to be the son of Aphrodite the Mother
and to be the son of Aphrodite the Mother is to be Greek
and to be Greek is to be ancient
and to be ancient is to be pre-historic
and to be pre-historic is to be mythological
and to be mythological is to be a Trojan prince
and to be a Trojan prince is to be a son of a shepherd
and to be a son of a shepherd is to be a son of Zeus
and to be a son of Zeus is to be descended from Titans
and to be descended from Titans is to be a god
and to be a god is to be divinely human
and to be divinely human is to be pre-Adamite
and to be pre-Adamite is to be shaped from particles of dust
and to be shaped from particles of dust is to be a scion of stars.

Foundation

Unable to stand in our hillside orchard,
too weak to swing a mattock or to wrestle

with dirt, my dad wants to plant peach trees.
For him, I tear the earth open.

Rocks bleed out from the poor mountain soil,
and I unwrap swaddled peach roots.

Before I scrape the dirt back and tamp it down,
I return the largest rock under the young roots,

a surrogate for what I fear. I bury it back,
imagine the roots encircling the rock,

enclosing it, building from its foundation.
Like the hard stone buried in the sweetest fruit.

Camel's Back

when the curve was deep and my father said he felt us tilt to two
    wheels
when my mother thought she left her purse at home
when he said *Easy*, like I was his horse
when I turned the radio on and he turned it off
when she pointed to the ninth lilac bush
when he called the man waiting for the crosswalk sign *a peasant*
    because of his large straw hat
when conversation turned to the election
when the seat belt began to strangle me like a rope on a spring steer
when he read the billboard for the *lady psychic* as the *lady psycho*
when he crumpled the loose lid on the large cup and golden-brown
    tea splashed across his shirt
when she lost her lip balm somewhere in the backseat
when she thought she left her purse at the doctor's office
when I drove through the yellow light
when I stopped at the yellow light
when the conversation split into two but only one of us realized it
when the air conditioner blew too cold, too hard, too loud, too much
when it started to rain and he reminded me the road is slickest when
    it's newly wet
when he said *Easy, Easy, Easy*, for the last time

Standing on the Banks of the Tuckasegee

I'm told the First People had no words
for wilderness, no concept of separation
from the land—not in body or spirit.

Even in death, the flesh was given
to the ground like an apple seed
before winter snows.

                    If not wilderness,
what to call this rough country
that devours me and all of us tasked
to dig the hole and plant the seed?

In this wilderness, gray skies dull
daylight hours. Heaving rains fall.
Rivers swell, reclaim valley floor.

There's no loam left to plow and plant,
no soil for a seed to take root,
and the seed is not a seed.

The Fence Builder

My graves don't rise or sink
the grave digger says after I show him

the place to bury my father.
I take in the view as if this valley

is what he'll see for eternity.
Down the hill, children play

outside the elementary school.
Sheep pasture around the cemetery.

Some people just push their pile of dirt back in.
But I tamp the dirt at every level.

I'd never wondered why some graves swell
and some settle and sag

but the grave digger's words stay with me.
He taps the clay above my sleeping dad,

leveling the damp ground
just as the man in the casket

taught me to tamp around wooden posts
to make a new fence last,

packing the dirt and rocks
so wire is pulled taut, forced to hold tight

for at least a generation,
those rhythmic strikes a refrain

for all who take pride in a task well done,
those men who work the earth—

the fence builder erecting his monuments,
the grave digger and all he lays to rest.

Balefire

The crimson king maple blows
in high winds, burns with October's
beautiful death. Before my disbelieving eyes,
leaves piled at the tree's base form
wings, take flight and fall upwards.
A reversal of everything I know.
These small, light birds flash
grayish white undersides
before disappearing into
the crimson king's flames.

Maybe they are
what field guides call
confusing fall warblers.
Maybe they are
some kind of finch,
but there are too many species
for my untrained eye.
Peterson's doesn't state
which birds have enough magic
to fly into fire.
Science is silent on why
some blazes appear as signal beacons
though they were built
as funeral pyres.

There is a barn

in this poem, built by men
a century ago—no one alive
remembers exactly, but someone
cut the oaks and sawed the planks,
nailed tin sheets to shape the roof.
This barn sits by a creek. Some springs,
the creek overflows and the barn floods.
There is a hay loft in this barn
and many poles between the rafters
where tobacco once hung to cure.
Gaps between the boards let fresh air enter.
Below the loft, the barn is divided into stables.
Horse tack still hangs in some
though no one alive remembers those horses.
Out of hard labor, calves have been born here
and died. So, too, womb-locked mothers.
In the last stall, a man I knew
stacked square hay bales as tight as mice,
though the hay was thick with thistles.
The following fall, the cattle were sold,
the pastures left fallow. The man died
and the hay moldered. Did I mention
this barn is black? Its roof too.
The man who packed the hay picked the paint
though there were red barns in his history.
Perhaps the barn's color doesn't matter
except to me because that man was my father.
God alone knows if it makes any difference
the hay was wasted by all but the mice,
always burrowing through the past.

Cows Don't Consider Oblivion

with apologies to Kevin Young

They obey the farmer and his fences
    when they're forced

and the dull hunger of their four stomachs.
    They lust only to pasture

in lush fields and to drink from a cool creek.
    They see little beyond

their meadow, longing for nothing
    more pleasing

than what's on the other side of the fence.
    But they don't fear

whether the world will continue without them.
    The future is a foreign notion.

They don't graze with the purpose
    of making a lasting mark.

They don't worry what will be written
    on their gravestones,

that the only inscription for their lives
    will be written

in the scattering of their bones.

Blue November

There's no blue like the sky in the eleventh
month. The woods know this, bare arms
of beech, sycamore lifted to blue vault,
reaching for help from Heaven. The wrens
know this as they hop, skitter across lawns,
under boxwood and juniper anchoring
flower beds, in and out of barn eaves.

The fox squirrel knows. He gathers acorns,
walnuts, the last hickories, surveys
his kingdom from throne of oak
fence post, weathered over decades,
smooth now as fossil memory. Almost

Thanksgiving. A single birdsfoot
violet blossoms in the pasture, hidden
in weeds, born out of season, waiting
for the killing frost. Night comes.
The moon is low and round, the third
this autumn—a blue moon, a harvest
moon. It charges forward, a wild
horse whose reins you've dropped.

You don't need to watch the squirrel
gather acorns. The same knowledge
is inside you—how to recognize
the blue moon by the angle it hangs.
There's no blue like lonesomeness
when the wind blows cold on your bare
arms reaching for help from Heaven.

Moonlight, especially November's
variety, is the falsest light.

Hag Stone, Hex Stone, Holy Stone

The farmer enters the mouth of the barn. In shadow
he palms the weathered oak beam above the stable door,
feels for a rusty nail to hang a string of baling twine,
the other end threaded to a rock with an eye in its center—
a natural hole, created by the witchery of water
boring through the stone over time. Hag stone,
hex stone, holy stone to save his cattle from bad dreams
while they're pendulous with unborn calves.

He bids his cows goodnight, trades barn dark
for the widening maw of dusk. In his own bed,
he counts the years he rifled dry riverbanks, seeking
a stone with enough magic to lock so many perils
in its threshold. And for peace to ease his own sleep,
to wash away his fears of midnight births, twisted
hooves, calves turned backwards, sideways.
Of umbilical cords wrapped around necks like nooses.

After My Father Died, I Marveled

In the field / cattle grazed, unbothered by the coming / winter, unfazed by the farmer's absence. / Chickens laid eggs. Phoebes darted / from post to post. / I ached with hunger— / the drive-through ladies kept taking / my orders, kept taking my money. On roadsides / deputies watched / men in striped safety vests /gather trash. / I drove back and forth / from my house to my father's house even though / he wasn't there. / Beside me on the road / teachers were driving to teach / and bankers driving to banks. Construction crews / built new homes, and real estate agents / listed and showed them / to new homeowners. Brokers / traded stocks and bonds. Cattle futures / skyrocketed. Advertisers and stores / rolled out Christmas campaigns and children / wrote letters to Santa, but / I was too spent / to cry or be angry / or feel anything except / the motion of it all.

A Dream with Deer

These trees where deep woods open
to field and light are so still
it's easy to believe nothing
of magnitude could happen here
—then three does
enter this limb-roofed church,
this sanctuary of frost-worn ground.
A wind with purpose blows
through last year's leaves,
loosening acorns like heavy rain.
The deer know this place,
and are unafraid of the wind
and swaying oaks, the acorns falling
like small but infinite offerings.
They bow their sleek heads and feast,
their muzzles moving fast and silent as prayer.

The Mystery of the Hereafter

after the sculpture by Augustus Saint-Gaudens

Do not call it Grief
even if grief is all you see.

It was meant to ask a question
not to give an answer

said the husband who paid the artist
to shape the shrouded figure

molded from clay, then forged in fire
to mark the grave of the wife who drank

her photo chemicals, the taste
of death as pungent as bitter almonds.

Which was more genius—
the inspiration or the execution

to give a bronze face to Nirvana—
beyond both joy and sorrow,

neither man nor woman,
with water-like robe and hood

flowing over the inscrutable
mystery of life and death.

I hear you, Henry Adams:
Do not call it Grief.

But I confess. Grief is all I see.

Remembered by Name

for Lee Smith

Chocolate: half Jersey, half Angus, the color
of milk mixed with magic. She was the first
calf my dad agreed was solely mine, a lesson
in responsibility. We bottle fed her, raised her
as a pet. For seventeen years, she scurried
from far pastures whenever I called. The spring
after she died, I propped her sun-bleached skull
on a rock wall overlooking our home in the hollow.

Abby: Chocolate's daughter. Allergic to weeds—
thistledown, sweet Joe Pye, ironweed—
we could hear her wheeze before we picked out
her sleek black back between those of her sisters.
Sold before winter for the exact amount of four
new car tires. One of Dad's hard lessons.

Eros: a mother in troubled childbirth, heaving,
too tired to scare away. My dad tied a noose
around the calf's tiny, protruding hooves.
Midwifery is easier when the mother stands
still, but when my dad pulled, Eros stormed.
Mom and I grabbed rope, and Eros drug three
of us across our eighty acres until Dad pinned
a foot against a fence post, held us until her calf
plopped to the ground, gained breath.

Baby: a dirty yellow Jersey, she looked like nothing
more than loosely connected bones. She never learned
to wean any of her calves, so sometimes, we found
two or more daughters drinking all at once. My dad
never saw her without wishing his grandma Susie Baker
was alive so he could give her a cow with so much milk.

Ellie: solidly, innocently white, whose lifeless body
I twice chased buzzards away from. I nursed her
with milk in a Ziplock bag, taught her to walk, forced
first steps until she was strong enough to walk alone.
She became my own child, and she loved me more
than her mother, at least for one single day of our lives.

Henry Beauclerk: the gentle red giant, sire of many
calves. Even my dad regretfully agreed Henry looked
sad when loaded on the trailer to be sold at market.
Many believe bulls are brutes, dumb and dangerous,
but Henry's eyes were soft and wet, as if he knew
he would never come home again.

Upon Meeting Judith Light in a Dream

What I wanted to say was how I grew up
watching *Who's the Boss*, how my mother
thought she was beautiful and I agreed,
the way her blond hair darkened at the skull.
I wanted to tell her I loved her in *Ugly Betty*,
that I wished she was on television more,
that she was still beautiful, especially
perhaps in my dream because of how dreams
bring the past back to life.

But the words that spilled out were instead
about my cousin, Michael, how he was:
the funniest human I've ever known,
how he watched *Titanic* twelve times in the theatre,
how he imitated voices and lines from movies,
how he wanted more literal band names arguing
for The Thom Yorke Band over Radiohead.
What exactly is a Radiohead? he said.
I told Judith how he played music by ear,
how the minister at his funeral said,
Michael Jones was a song.
I repeat those words every time I think of him,
which is so often, even a decade after.

I tried to tell Judith I was only two
the year the show broadcast, but later, I watched
her pivotal scene when, playing the respectable
doctor's wife, she reveals on the witness stand
that she's a prostitute.

Reader, it might sound tawdry to you,
maybe a little humorous if you're young
and can't imagine the ways we were restricted
only forty years ago, the lengths we all took
to hide our true natures. I wanted to thank
Judith Light for giving voice to a character
with low self-esteem, dissatisfied, forced
to split herself in two—too much pressure
when we each only have our own one life.

Play Where I'm Cast as Sycorax

When it was time
to act the raven
and pack my father
into his final strongbox,
I chose an acorn
that towered,
with him inside,
into an oak
with gently-
furrowed, ivy-
covered bark.
His heart
beats there
inside leaves
glimmering
in sunlight,
golden-green
as hummingbird
feathers,
on branches
reaching
heavenward
like
fists.

On the Other Side of Wilderness

We lowered our heads
in sorrow and disappeared
into the tall woods
without hatchet or arrows.
We taught ourselves to not leave
tracks among the pine
needles and stinging nettles,
learned killing a wolf
brought revenge from other wolves.
We learned to taste disease.

*

In January
Venus will reign in the sky.
On the other side
of wilderness, we will see
that last year's sorrows belong
to last year, that we're
embryo inside acorn,
wind inside the wind.
And earth's dirt—though dark and damp—
will be more garden than grave.

Maelstrom

Where's my mother in this vortex of grief?
I see her boat still upright, still afloat,

but I'm bailing so much murky water.
I'm watching my hull and the puncture there—

aperture of my pain-eye—
that swells and constricts like it's alive.

The sea around us swirls, wrenches us
perilously toward the pull of the undertow.

For now, it's enough to share the hurtling
water, waving white flags as we circle,

waiting for this whirlpool to loose its hold.
One less than three, we bob along

on the surges, but my sorrow
feels whalesome and wholly my own.

If there's an angel of lost gloves

my father didn't believe and didn't wait
for holy intercession. He mislaid his gloves
faster than his temper. He wasn't careless,

though I never knew him to lay hands
on the tool he needed when he needed it.
So he bought pair after pair, suede

cowhide fit to stretch barbed wire. Still,
he usually worked with only one hand
sheathed and sometimes then

with the fingers blown out, each digit
ruptured by the snag of steel points
reaching next to rip open skin.

Now, I find his leather fingers cupping air
like wren nests, lingering in buckets,
on shed shelves, on the aged oak floor

of the barn loft, in the midst of a task,
maybe a pair of nails within reach,
as if he'll return when he finds his hammer.

II

The Eyes of God

after Felix Pollak

Nightly, he dreams of flying in a car over a city of gabled roofs.

Obviously, you're in need of money, says his broker.

Such a show off, says his ex-wife. *Can't you dream about regular cars like a normal person?*

His mechanic thinks only of practical matters. He wants to know if the brakes work in the air, and how's the power steering?

Your head's always in the clouds, says his boss.

Clearly, your life is out of control, says his older sister.

His therapist says it's a good sign, that he will rise above his current troubles.

But not even the therapist asks him where he flies each night and who he's with. So the dreamer never reveals the car is one of his dad's old convertibles, and that his dad, dead now more than a year, is the driver. He doesn't describe the joy they both feel sailing through the air over this endless city. He doesn't tell how beautiful and intricate the roofs are, that the gables are layered in aged copper, their patina a sign of something old and lasting, their elaborate designs usually reserved only for the eyes of God.

We Are Called to Reinvent Ourselves

It takes so little to become disoriented
when walking in the woods. I attempt
to retrace my path home, but the trail moves
or I do   and in a flash, I forget all I should know.

Light romances its way through the tree canopy,
travels on branches, stipples against bark.

Flickers of blue might be feathers,
are more likely slips of sky.
Singing birds hidden in the leaves
refuse to reveal themselves.

The log fallen long ago is a dun-colored buck
standing stone still, hind quarters glistening.

You can spend a lifetime memorizing a place,
the trails and trees, the land's lay and water's flow,
dividing your dreams from those
who walked there before you.

It is the shank of the day,
but is it the foreshank or the hindshank?

Roots

The tree roots withered
the year after my father died.
Not under trees still reaching and green—
but all the roots that remained
in the ground from all the trees
he'd cut over the decades.
My dad was a devil with a chainsaw.
That first year, I did a lot of walking
and a lot of falling into the unexpected
divots, each one a simple depression
exactly the size of a man's footstep.

Here was a line of pear trees.
This hemlock grew too close to the barn.
Lightning struck this apple. This cherry
stopped bearing fruit. In a season,
their roots all rotted away,
their absence another reminder
of who had stood in that place.

Learning to Drive

Sundays after church, after miles of my pleading,
my dad turned onto the gravel lane at the mouth
of our hollow. He and I switched places,
my mom already relegated to the back seat.
Dad confessed to be a hillbilly only in one way—
he collected more cars than we could drive—
ancient Cadillacs you could float down river,
a Chevy Celebrity the color and size of an army tank,
and, my favorite, a brown '79 Ford Thunderbird
that once plowed through four feet of snow
in a blizzard. I remember the Ford's slick,
hard plastic steering wheel, the shining metal
of the gear handle pulled down to Drive.
The V8 surged forward before my foot touched
the gas. Mom complained, said don't jerk the car.
Dad hushed her, waved me on. I swerved
around potholes, paused at the top of the hill
for Dad to count his cows in the pasture, hugged
the bank to let a neighbor pass, inching us
closer to our driveway, adding a half mile
every Sunday, to the odometer that someday
would take me anywhere but back home.

A Quarrelsome Old Couple Lives in My Dreams

One says the witch stone in the cow shed sweetens the milk.
The other swears the stone lets the calves fall easy as silk.

Violet Iris

Why are you always the first to flower?
Did the gods send you to blaze the trail
for others to follow?
Twenty thousand years ago—longer—
it was your color men sought,
grinding manganese and hematite powder
with a dab of animal fat
to capture wild cattle on cave walls.

Even before we drew our dreams in stone,
you budded and bloomed, unfurled
soft daggers of falling petals before your yellow,
white and rusted sisters.
Now, I beg you.
Linger. Take off your shoes. Some tulips
and the last few daffodils are still laid up
in their beds, lazing away the spring
while you become violet bruise of memory.

In the spring flood's rushing, water sweeps out

the old foundation stones. In a flash, the walls of the farm's last barn follow.
Like a prayer, my mother asks, what will happen to all the swallows?

The Broken Man

after a photograph by Terry Price, for the Ekphrastic Poetry Project,
Czech Republic Edition

At the base of Petřín Hill, seven
broken men stand, bronze sentinels.

One man has a terrible tear down the middle,
exactly the place a doctor

would hold the stethoscope to count
the beats of the heart not there. A hunk

of his skull is missing, too, and his left eye—
but he's more whole than most of his brothers.

His right eye still sits in its socket
though it's turned away from the crowd

and away from the photographer: a man
who tells his son not to be afraid to grasp

the broken man's long, bronze fingers
with his own small hands. The statue refuses

to gaze at the boy, at this 21st century
Wenceslaus dressed in the Republic's

colors, a child who will imagine
broken men becoming whole again,

the miracle and magic of
the dead breathed back to life.

The Sherpa Jacket

My friend's new jacket jolts me back to 1981
and one just like it my dad wore—
faded denim, sherpa-lined. *Is it vintage?* I ask
but he says no, it's new from JC Penney.
Sure enough, the same waist-length Levi's jacket
is online, only $98 "for the urban cowboy look."

A year after his passing,
twenty-some years since he wore it last,
the jacket still hangs in his closet,
mine when I want it—

When I was five, I believed
sherpa's fuzzy naps were real lamb's wool.
I'd crawl inside the jacket, get warm, fall asleep.
That was the year we lived in Kentucky
in the mining camp where my dad was raised,
where the floors stayed cold
no matter how hard the furnace churned.
We left after that winter,
his parents' ghosts too much to live with.

The Abacist

I remember that man well
who sat with an abacus, unendingly
patient—one of those men
who counted tobacco sheaths,
casks of wine and rice paddies
as easily as he tallied
quantities of grain in the shadows
of the great pyramids—
his fine, nimble fingers
sliding stones over a board of sand.

No one knew the truth of his past.
He had been born on an island.
He watched the ibis
wade the marsh for crustaceans.
He believed the ibis
gifted man with mathematics,
the moon and magic.
So he counted the birds like
seers count crows, computing
meaning beyond their numbers.

On clear nights, he counted stars
until his eyelids grew too heavy
to stay awake. In dreams,
he counted lost loves, their nights
together and nights apart
growing like twin-row crops
in the same acre of ache.

Conventional wisdom says
we count to remember
the details of our existence.
The abacist knew
we often count to forget—

Whatever Frame It Pleases

The ruby-throated hummingbird
weighs less than an acorn—
its beating heart lighter still—yet it flies
without rest across the Gulf of Mexico.
My father's soul weighed less than a feather.
How far did he need to travel to transcend,
to transform into whatever's next?
Ovid said *nothing dies, the spirit wanders.*
So I dream my father into acorn and then oak.
I dream him into hummingbird and then star.
The spirit *never perishes*, and new stars are born
from nothing more than hydrogen, gravity and time—

Fishing with the Saint

I quit fishing long ago; it's a lot of staring at the deep,
but I gather rod and net again and warily cast a line,
counting fish like sheep in restless sleep;
I pray the sainted lady stays always by my side.

All I catch are common bream too small to save.
I send them back to the mud, careful not to clutch
their sharp and spiny fins. How many times must I wade
from the water leaving blood on all I touch?

After reading her visions, it's not Lady Hildegard
but my own holy mother who fills my dreams.
She releases fish, one by one, coating them in sacred
oil before she bequeaths them back into the breach.

From further up the mountainous shore,
I see her standing in early morning mist.
I call to her, over and over—Mother! Mother!
She calls back only when she needs more oil, more fish.

Fresh as an Asteraceae

I'm full of bad habits. I build walls,
murder my own dreams. I forget
to trust myself. I forget simple facts.

Did you know the almond
is not a true nut but the seed
of a drupe, which is a fruit
like a peach or a plum or a cherry?

The almond is a kernel buried within
the pit, like the pharaoh is the kernel
in the sarcophagus of the pyramid,
like the divine ka—our vital spark
—resides, while we breathe,
in our beating hearts.

Did you know daisies
open each dawn and close at night?
Their name literally means
Day's Eye. Did you know

you can rid yourself of shame, of hate?
I am doing it, or I am trying.
I am tilling new ground,
one fistful of daisy seeds
at a time. I am getting fresh legs
and breathing fresh air.
I am fresh as a star.

Here's another fact. Did you know
the sky is a dun-colored cow
with soft eyes and heavy lids, the stars
freshly painted each night on her underbelly?

Spring Signs

Needleless, the beetle-eaten pine stood
through its last snow but fell in seedtime winds.

The weary vixen moved her three fox kits
into the old groundhog hole behind the barn.
Yesterday, they wrestled in weak afternoon heat.

Days ago, the Christmas kitten climbed up
the walnut but was afraid to climb back down.
Today, she killed a baby grey squirrel.

                Death, even in spring.

Another frost is sure to fall, maybe more than one,
but the apples bloom. Dogwoods and redbuds too.

Copperhead

Dead: the copperhead
that slipped down the ridge
in summer's elongated dusk
to forage small prey
and taste cool creek. And me,
racing against the sun
on its path beyond the mountains
to end my task mowing tall grass
between apples, pears and peaches.

Before the snake, I had been looking
without resentment at the day
well spent, a day devoted
to necessary labor. Later, memory
of cold blood spilled on steel blades
lingered in the night air
like honeysuckle and regret.

Purification

Because I couldn't abide the fire, I chose water / but the river / is designed equally for baptism / and drowning. / For a day, a week, a month I fell / downstream / while the rapids churned in ecstasy. / Parts of me flaked off / like brook trout / and swam upstream. / What remained of me / beached on an island. I was afraid / to re-enter the water. / So I rested my head on a rock / like Jacob. I dreamed myself / into a monk's habit / shaped the island into a house of worship / with an altar / built from rabbit bones. / A week, a month, a year passed / while I waited. I tried to decipher / the divinations of katydids, crickets, cicadas / those oldest prophets—but their ruckus / was drowned out by the rush of water / the flow and gurgle, the turbulent push and pull / of rock and rapid / forever / coursing downstream.

Riding Lawn Mower

After the first small-engine repairman
tells me five miles is too far for a house call
or a pick up, the second repairman tells me
I should disassemble the mower myself,
bring him the offending portion.

Lincoln said his father taught him to work
but never to like it. My father taught me
to work on lawn mowers. So of course,
I think about buying a new machine.

Instead, I crawl onto summer-warm grass
like my father taught me. I pull
S-pins and retaining springs, freeing
suspension arms and the anti-sway bar,
separating clutch rod from clutch lever.
I mechanic my way beyond my skill set
until the mulching deck falls limp.

A pneumatic drill unlocks frozen, broken
blades turned upside down. New ones
hex bolt on, naked edges glinting in the light.
I reverse engineer, reattach metal to metal,
secure it all with a taut pulley belt.

Such unbindings and rebindings are common.
This tractor and I will again tame briar hells
of blackberry, wild rose. We will battle stones
rising quietly in the pasture at night like ghosts.

There is no choice but to keep going,
to keep working until the final, unfixable end.

Unburied

Slick with summer, my father's cattle lumber
over hills, their rounded bellies full of grass
and unborn calves. They watch as I follow
fence lines, wonder how the strong barbed
wire breaks, how the briar hells overtake
once clean rows. I hack the blackberries
and the wild rose, patch the strands of wire
the way my father taught me. I cut cedar
saplings at their base, clear the pastures
of fallen tree limbs. Of cow bones, too—
unburied by wild dogs and packs of coyotes
that howl in the night—hungering for flesh,
finding all that's left is bone.

My Mother Is the Green Mountains

My mother is the Green Mountains
grinding against the horizon. She built
the wall at the end of the world.

She is the pilgrim's narrow path
cut through violet fields of wildflowers.
My mother is the Green Mountains

discharging many winged congregations
from her ancient rocky arms.
The wall at the end of the world

is where we watch the zigzagging lights
of fireflies meld into distant stars.
My mother is the Green Mountains

afflicted by invisible danger
riding on the wings of mosquitoes
to the wall at the end of the world.

She is everyone I love, no longer with me.
She is a dream that can't be recaptured.
My mother is the Green Mountains,
the wall at the end of the world.

South Through Kentucky

The yellow moon rides low, expectant as a summer melon
to light my way through places our longhunter forefathers

named: Madison, Rockcastle, Laurel. Off the interstate,
the moon roosts among emblems for fast food & vacant hotels.

Further South, I pass Gray, Bailey's Switch, Bimble,
the three acres where your grandparents lived their last years.

Each mile past Flat Lick and the Narrows grows closer to home.
Always ahead, the moon hangs before me like a greedy owl,

tracking what I can't yet see. On the other side of the mountain,
the moon with the harvest flair transforms to shining bone-

white orb. I decide there must be two moons:
one in the country of your youth, one here to mark your grave.

The Topography of Tears

As a boy, I cried despite my father's warnings—I was too old, boys don't cry, crying does no good, it solves no problems. Scientists categorize tears this way: basal tears to lubricate and nourish; reflex tears to protect from irritants like wind and smoke; and psychic tears produced as an emotional response. I wish I had known as a boy that hormones in psychic tears work as natural pain killers. An analgesic for what ails you.

After my father died, I discovered Rose-Lynn Fisher's microscopic images of tears titled and displayed like exhibits in a museum: *Tears from Onions*, *Tears of Grief*, *Tears of Change*, *Tears of Ending & Beginning*.

Tears of Grief resembles an unfinished map, a cartographer's abandoned plat. Of all the slides, *Tears of Grief* forms the straightest lines, like fragments of roads in a city only half planned.

I could never stop crying just because my father ordered it. Once the sluice opened, the water rushed through, became its own master, the mechanism easier to start than stop. The disappointment in his eyes made me cry harder.

I wish I'd understood then that we cry every time we blink, every moment of our lives; it's the first act we perform when we're born. As a species, humans had the ability to cry before we developed language skills. What better proof is there of the infinite sadness of the human condition?

My high school science teacher described water as sticky because it clings to everything it touches. Think of trees dashed by a downpour: the water doesn't rush off the leaves. It lingers. Think how water clings to our bodies. Think how tears grip our skin, hanging on, drop by drop, until the weight becomes unbearable—enough to form a lake deep enough for drowning.

When my father died, my uncles stood unbelieving sentries around his open casket, searching the stone face for something already departed. They cried when I could not. A microscopic slide of nothing must resemble a desert landscape with only barren flats on the horizon. My eyes were two cracked millstones, too broken to grind grain, too fractured to kill pain.

Life without my father felt like an alternate dimension. I remembered how to cry only after the others left—the uncles and cousins and well-wishing neighbors. Their well-meant memories muddled the silence I needed to re-envision my world. My loss was like a seed waiting for the proper conditions to break open.

I returned to Fisher's slides and learned they are art not science, the tears manipulated in myriad ways. Some air-dried, some compressed. Even the volume of tears placed on the slide changes the experience, the same way a skiff in summer mist sails differently than in a squall. In the editing process, the artist blurred and sharpened, clarified areas of unwanted softness, contrasted the colors and tones, zooming in on a detail of the whole, until something began to feel recognizable among the random chaos. Her deliberate variations changed the images, mirroring the different reasons we cry.

There's little reliable science about how emotional tears might alter from person to person or from one passion to another. But I like the idea that no single tear is like any other.

I imagine hanging photos of my own tears on the walls of a gallery, naming each one to correspond to the events of their creation: *Tears of Connection Broken, Tears of Hindsight, Tears of Recollection, Tears of Reconstruction*. Each of my tears is strikingly different. My favorite depicts a shoreline with a sturdy dock where brave boats embark into mapless, swirling seas.

Notes

Genealogy, page 6: the structure of this poem is inspired by Major Jackson's "OK Cupid."

Standing on the Banks of the Tuckasegee, page 10: this poem was written while visiting the Tuckasegee River near Dillsboro, North Carolina. The Cherokee commonly refer to themselves as the first people.

There is a barn, page 14: this poem was inspired by Jennifer Stewart Miller's poem, *This poem has a highway in it*, published in her 2021 collection, *Thief*.

Blue November, page 16: a "blue moon" is a fairly infrequent phenomenon involving the appearance of an additional full moon within a given period.

The Mystery of the Hereafter, page 20: Augustus Saint-Gaudens' famous cast bronze sculpture was commissioned by author and historian Henry Adams as a memorial for his wife, Marian "Clover" Hooper Adams.

Upon Meeting Judith Light in a Dream, page 24: this poem is dedicated to the memory of my cousin and friend, Michael Jones.

Play Where I'm Cast as Sycorax, page 26: Sycorax, an unseen character in William Shakespeare's *The Tempest*, is an ancient witch who imprisoned the sprite Ariel in a tree. Her name is roughly translated as "the Scythian raven."

On the Other Side of Wilderness, page 27: the structure of this poem is a somonka, a Japanese form of poetry.

If there's an angel of lost gloves, page 29: this poem is inspired by a photograph taken by Justin Hamm: justinhamm.net/photography.

The Broken Man, page 40: this poem is inspired by a photograph taken by Terry Price of The Memorial to the Victims of Communism, a series of statues in Prague commemorating the victims of the communist era between 1948 and 1989.

South Through Kentucky, page 56: "longhunter" is a reference to the 18th-century explorers and hunters who made expeditions into the Kentucky frontier wilderness for as much as six months at a time.

Thanks

The poems in this volume would not exist if not for the generous reading and thoughtful critique, not to mention the friendship, of Emily Mohn-Slate, Joanne Proulx, Cassie Pruyn, and Jennifer Stewart Miller.

Thanks to Charlie and Mary Allen, Bobby Amburgey, Darnell Arnoult, Wesley and Valetta Browne, Donna Crow, Scott Douglass and Main Street Rag, Robert Gipe, Jesse Graves, Jay Hodges, Major Jackson, Keith Lesmeister, Davin Malasarn, Tony Maxwell, Carrie Mullins, Walter Robinson, Shawna Kay Rodenberg, Rosemary Rhodes Royston, Cindy Stephenson who gave me a physical space to write, Tiffany Williams, Joe Wolfenbarger, Sylvia Woods, and especially my mother Karen Loving.

Thanks to the supportive communities of the Bennington Writing Seminars, the Key West Literary Seminar and Writers' Workshop Program, the Eckerd College Writers' Conference: Writers in Paradise, and the Sewanee Writers' Conference.

Thanks to Marc Jolley, Marsha Luttrell, Jenny Toole, Mary Beth Kosowski, and Jessica Moore at Mercer University Press for believing in my work.